$ 19.95

# Big Time Rush

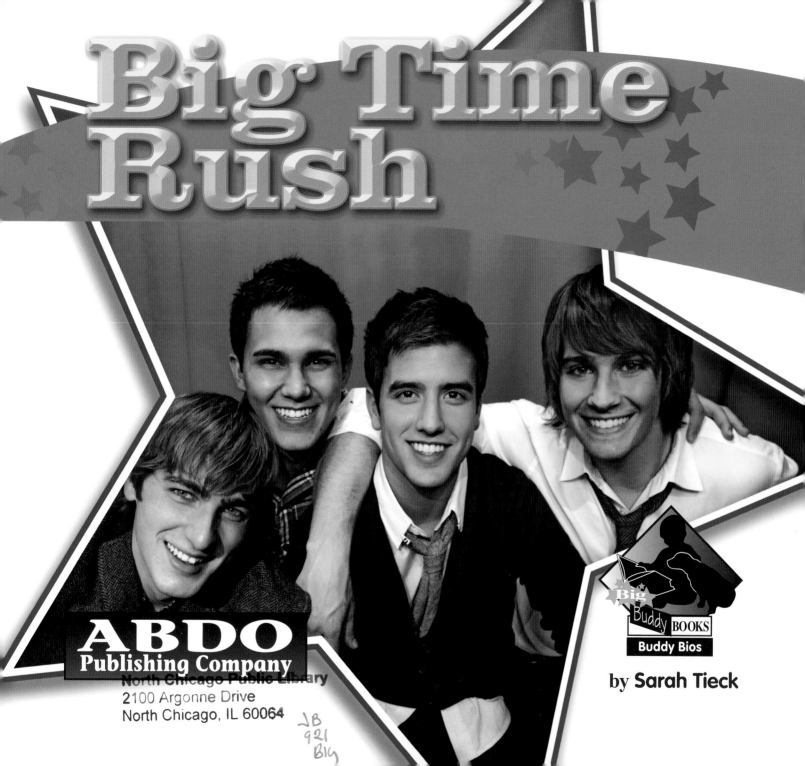

by **Sarah Tieck**

Big Buddy BOOKS
**Buddy Bios**

## VISIT US AT
**www.abdopublishing.com**

Published by ABDO Publishing Company, PO Box 398166, Minneapolis, Minnesota 55439.

Copyright © 2014 by Abdo Consulting Group, Inc. International copyrights reserved in all countries. No part of this book may be reproduced in any form without written permission from the publisher. Big Buddy Books™ is a trademark and logo of ABDO Publishing Company.

Printed in the United States of America, North Mankato, Minnesota.
052013
092013

 PRINTED ON RECYCLED PAPER

Coordinating Series Editor: Rochelle Baltzer
Contributing Editors: Megan M. Gunderson, Marcia Zappa
Graphic Design: Maria Hosley
Cover Photograph: *AP Photo*: Seth Wenig.
Interior Photographs/Illustrations: *AP Photo*: Carlo Allegri (p. 5), Tammie Arroyo (p. 11), fls (p. 9), Chris Pizzello (p. 15), Rex Features via AP Images (p. 17), T. Sakakibara (p. 9), PRNewsFoto/Nickelodeon/Stewart Shining (p. 7), Katy Winn/Invision (p. 19); *Getty Images*: Brian Ach (p. 13), Imeh Akpanudosen (p. 21), Adam Bettcher/Getty Images for Nickelodeon (p. 27), C Flanigan/FilmMagic (p. 25), Frazer Harrison (p. 23), Chelsea Lauren (p. 29), Michael Loccisano/Getty Images for Nickelodeon (p. 24).

**Library of Congress Control Number: 2012923823**

**Cataloging-in-Publication Data**

Tieck, Sarah.
 Big Time Rush: popular boy band / Sarah Tieck.
  p. cm. -- (Big buddy biographies)
 ISBN 978-1-61783-856-9
 1. Big Time Rush--Juvenile literature. 2. Singers--United States--Biography--Juvenile literature. I. Title.
 782.42164092--dc23
 [B]                                                                          2012923823

# Big Time Rush

# Contents

# Rising Stars

Big Time Rush is a music group. Its members sing popular music. They also star in a television show called *Big Time Rush*. The boys appear in magazines. And, they have been guests on popular television shows.

Did you know...

Scott Fellows is a producer of
*Big Time Rush*. He had worked
with Carlos on a show called
*Ned's Declassified School
Survival Guide*.

# Big Break

Casting for *Big Time Rush* started in 2007. More than 1,500 people tried out! The show's **producers** wanted actors to star on a television show. But, they also wanted **performers** for a band.

Logan, James, Carlos, and Kendall were chosen. The band Big Time Rush officially formed in 2009 in Los Angeles, California.

Carlos plays Carlos Garcia. James's character is James Diamond. Logan plays Logan Mitchell. And, Kendall's character is Kendall Knight.

# Boy Band

Scott Fellows got the idea for Big Time Rush from a boy band called the Monkees. The Monkees formed around 1966. Like Big Time Rush, they starred in a television show.

The Monkees were one of the first boy bands. Over the years, many others have become very popular. These include New Kids on the Block and One Direction. Like these bands, Big Time Rush has some excited fans!

The Monkees members were Mike Nesmith (*top*), Davy Jones (*middle left*), Peter Tork (*middle right*), and Micky Dolenz (*bottom*).

"Daydream Believer" is one famous Monkees song.

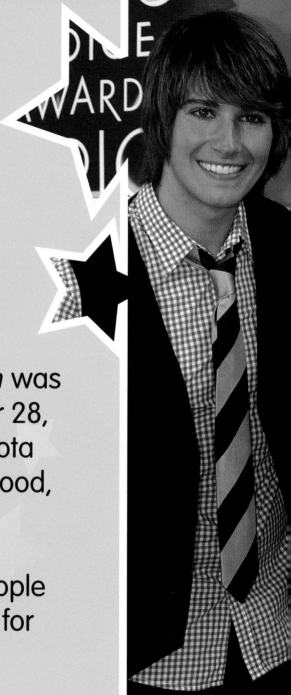

# Television Stars

The first **episode** of *Big Time Rush* was shown on Nickelodeon on November 28, 2009. The story is about four Minnesota hockey players. They move to Hollywood, California, to form a boy band.

The show's first season started on January 18, 2010. Nearly 7 million people watched that night! This set a record for Nickelodeon.

*Big Time Rush* quickly became popular in the United States and Europe.

# First Album

While filming their show, Big Time Rush made an album. They worked hard recording songs and videos. They practiced for hours!

In October 2010, Big Time Rush **released** *BTR*. It included songs from the show. "Boyfriend" and "Worldwide" were two of their most popular songs.

# Growing Talent

Big Time Rush became very popular! In 2011, the band released its second album. It is called *Elevate*. Hit songs include "Music Sounds Better with U" and "If I Ruled the World."

The television show was also successful. The boys continued filming more episodes. And in 2012, they starred in *Big Time Movie*. In this movie, the boys sing songs from the famous band the Beatles. A soundtrack was also released.

In 2012, Big Time Rush won a Nickelodeon Kids' Choice Award for Favorite Music Group.

Oklahoma

New Mexico

Arkansas

North Richland Hills

Louisiana

TEXAS

*GULF OF MEXICO*

MEXICO

# Music Lover

The members of Big Time Rush had not worked together before they **auditioned** for the show. Logan Phillip Henderson was born in Texas on September 14, 1989. He grew up in North Richland Hills in a family that loved music.

Logan wanted to act. In early 2008, he had a small part on the television show *Friday Night Lights*. Later that year, he moved to Los Angeles. Soon after, he was cast in *Big Time Rush*.

In his free time, Logan
likes to snowboard.

# Triple Threat

James David Maslow was born in New York City, New York, on July 16, 1990. He grew up in La Jolla, California.

At age six, James started training to be a singer. He attended special schools and learned to sing, act, and dance. People who have all three of these skills are called triple threats.

In 2008, James got a part on Nickelodeon's *iCarly*. The next year, he was chosen for *Big Time Rush*.

James is the tallest member of Big Time Rush. He is more than six feet (1.8 m) tall!

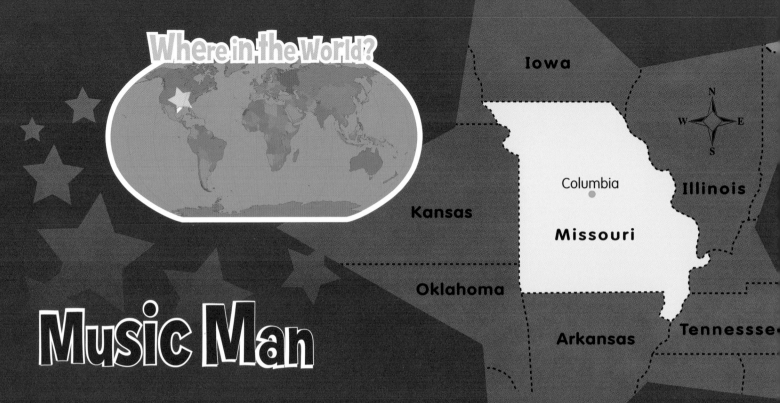

## Music Man

Carlos Roberto Pena Jr. was born in Columbia, Missouri, on August 15, 1989. He grew up in Weston, Florida. He was a cheerleader in school. He also appeared in musicals such as *Grease*.

Starting at age 15, Carlos had small parts on *ER* and other television shows. After high school, he studied musical theater at the Boston Conservatory. Because of this, Carlos almost didn't audition for *Big Time Rush*.

Carlos, Logan, and Kendall made a video with Justin Bieber, Selena Gomez, and others. They pretended to sing "Call Me Maybe" by Carly Rae Jepsen. Carlos posted it on YouTube.

Carlos is Spanish, Venezuelan, and Dominican.

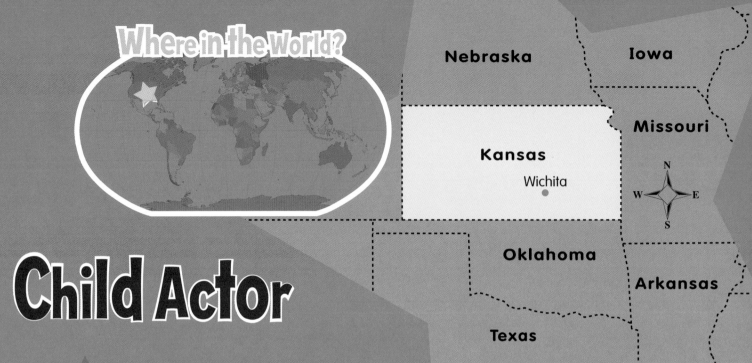

# Child Actor

Kendall Francis Schmidt was born in Wichita, Kansas, on November 2, 1990. He started acting at around age five.

By the time Kendall was about ten, he had moved to California. He had small parts on several television shows, including *Gilmore Girls* and *ER*.

In addition to Big Time Rush, Kendall is part of another band. It is called Heffron Drive. He writes songs, plays **guitar**, and sings.

Kendall was the last person chosen for *Big Time Rush*. On the show, he is considered the group's leader.

# Behind the Scenes

The members of Big Time Rush spend many hours practicing and recording music. They also learn **lines** and film scenes for their television show.

The boys go on tour and **perform** live concerts. When they are on tour, they live on buses. They travel to cities around the world. They also attend events and meet fans. Their fans are always excited to see them!

In 2012, Big Time Rush (*right*) and One Direction (*below*) toured together.

# Off the Stage

The members of Big Time Rush spend free time at home with their friends and families. They also like to help people in need. They worked with Fender Music Foundation to give away **guitars** to schools. And, they **perform** at events to raise money for certain causes.

Reporters often take pictures of the members of Big Time Rush. Fans ask for their autographs.

# Buzz

Opportunities for the members of Big Time Rush continue to grow. In June 2013, they **released** their third album. It is called *24/Seven*. Also in 2013, they filmed the fourth season of *Big Time Rush*. Fans are excited to see what they'll do next!

In 2013, Big Time Rush performed with Victoria Justice as part of their Summer Break Tour.

# Snapshot

⭐**Names**: Logan Phillip Henderson; James David Maslow; Carlos Roberto Pena Jr.; Kendall Francis Schmidt

⭐**Birthdays**: September 14, 1989 (Logan); July 16, 1990 (James); August 15, 1989 (Carlos); November 2, 1990 (Kendall)

⭐**Albums**: *BTR, Elevate, Big Time Movie Soundtrack, 24/Seven*

⭐**Appearances Together**: *Big Time Rush, Big Time Movie*

# Important Words

**audition** (aw-DIH-shuhn) to give a trial performance showcasing personal talent as a musician, a singer, a dancer, or an actor.

**episode** one show in a series of shows.

**guitar** (guh-TAHR) a stringed musical instrument played by strumming.

**lines** the words an actor says in a play, a movie, or a show.

**musical** a story told with music.

**perform** to do something in front of an audience. A performer is someone who performs.

**producer** a person who oversees the making of a movie, a play, an album, or a radio or television show.

**release** to make available to the public.

**soundtrack** a recording of the music featured in a movie or television show.

# Web Sites

To learn more about Big Time Rush, visit ABDO Publishing Company online. Web sites about Big Time Rush are featured on our Book Links page. These links are routinely monitored and updated to provide the most current information available.

## www.abdopublishing.com

# Index